WHAT DOES A
MIDFIELDER
DO?

Paul Challen

PowerKiDS
press.

New York

Published in 2018 by The Rosen Publishing Group, Inc.
29 East 21st Street, New York, NY 10010

Developed and Produced for Rosen by BlueApple*Works* Inc.
Managing Editor for BlueApple*Works*: Melissa McClellan
Art Director: Tibor Choleva
Designer: Joshua Avramson
Photo Research: Jane Reid
Editor: Marcia Abramson

Photo Credits: Cover left Olga Dmitrieva/Shutterstock; cover right Amy Myers/Shutterstock; title page, p. 8 Louis Horch/Dreamstime.com; TOC background, backgrounds p. 4, 8, 10, 14, 16, 20, 22, 26, 30, 32 romakoma/Shutterstock; TOC, p. 27 right Noah Salzman/Creative Commons; page numbers EFKS/Shutterstock; backgrounds; top backgrounds p. 4, 8, 10, 14, 16, 20, 22, 26 Christian Bertrand/Shutterstock; backgrounds 6, 7, 12, 13, 18, 19, 24, 25, 28, 29 odd-add/Shutterstock; p. 4, 5, 9 TJ Choleva; Page backgrounds odd-add/Shutterstock; p. 6 CLS Digital Arts/Shutterstock; p. 7 CP DC Press/Shutterstock; p. 10 Stef22/Dreamstime.com; p. 11 CHEN WS/Shutterstock; p. 12 barbsimages/Shutterstock; p. 13 Pukhov Konstantin/Shutterstock; p. 14 Peter Muzslay/Dreamstime.com; p. 15 Antonio Ros/Dreamstime.com; p. 16 CP DC Press/Shutterstock; p. 17 Robwilson39/Dreamstime.com; p. 18, 19, 21 muzsy/Shutterstock; p. 20 Marco Iacobucci EPP/Shutterstock; p. 21 top joshjdss/Creative Commons; p. 22 Vlad1988/Shutterstock; p. 23 Pukhov Konstantin/Shutterstock; p. 24 Stef22 /Dreamstime.com; p. 25 Paparazzofamily/Dreamstime.com; p. 26 left lev radin/Shutterstock; p. 26 right mr3002/Shutterstock; p. 27 left Mitch Gunn/Shutterstock; p. 27 top katatonia82/Shutterstock; p. 28 Katatonia82/Dreamstime.com; p. 29 Chris Van Lennep/Dreamstime.com; p. 29 top CP DC Press/Shutterstock; back cover Krivosheev Vitaly

Cataloging-in-Publication Data
Names: Challen, Paul.
Title: What does a midfielder do? / Paul Challen.
Description: New York : PowerKids Press, 2018. | : Soccer smarts | Includes index.
Identifiers: ISBN 9781508154518 (pbk.) | ISBN 9781508154471 (library bound) |
  ISBN 9781508154396 (6 pack)
Subjects: LCSH: Soccer-- literature.
Classification: LCC GV943.25 C53 2018 | DDC 796.334'64--dc23

Manufactured in China

CPSIA Compliance Information: Batch #BS17PK For Further Information contact: Rosen Publishing, New York, New York at 1-800-237-9932

CONTENTS

THE SOCCER TEAM

The game of soccer is played by two teams. Each team has 11 players. On each team, the goalkeeper is the one player who remains in the net and tries to keep the other team from scoring. The other 10 players are the defenders, midfielders, and forwards. Unlike many other sports, a soccer team can arrange their 10 outfield players in any **formation** it wants.

Soccer formations are described by using numbers, starting with the number of defenders, then the midfielders, and then the forwards. A common 4-4-2 formation means a team will play with four defenders, four midfielders, and two attacking forwards.

Forward

Forward

Outside Midfielder

Center Midfielder

Outside Back (Defender)

Outside Midfielder

Center Midfielder

Center Back (Defender)

Center Back (Defender)

Goalkeeper

Outside Back (Defender)

4-4-2 Formation

THE ROLE OF THE MIDFIELDER

Just as the name suggests, midfield players usually stay in the middle of the field. There are many different kinds of midfielders. Some like to hang back and help their team on defense, while others like to press forward and score or set up goals. The best midfielders combine both aspects of the game. Because they are always in the middle of the action, midfielders need to combine fast sprints with endurance. They are always some of the fittest players on their team.

The soccer field is also called the **pitch**. It is set up with two goals on either side. End lines run behind each goal, and sidelines run along the sides. Corner flags and markings are in each of the four corners. Each goal has a 6-yard box, a penalty spot, and an 18-yard box in front of it. The center circle is right in the middle of the field.

Corner Flag

Goal

Center Circle

Corner Flag

Penalty Spot

Goal

18-yard Box

Sideline

6-yard Box

End Line

Soccer Field

MIDFIELD UNIT

On a soccer team, midfielders work as a unit to control the middle of the pitch. Central midfielders stay close to the center of the field, while outside or wide midfielders play along the sidelines. Some midfielders are mainly defensive, **tackling** opposing players, winning the ball, and intercepting passes. Others play more offensively by dribbling, passing to set up goals, and even scoring themselves.

A good midfielder is also known as the team's "engine" because they power their team throughout the game. Whatever their exact position or job, it's important for midfielders to play as a unit. Soccer fans call this "keeping shape" because as the midfield unit moves up and down the field, it's important that its basic shape stays the same.

Since midfielders have a combination role of attack and defense, they play a very important part on a team. Midfielders are often the players with the strongest technical skills, such as dribbling and passing.

It's also important for midfielders to be good at **reading** the game because action takes place all around them. This takes what soccer coaches call a "high soccer IQ" — in other words, a lot of "game smarts" about how patterns of play develop on a soccer field.

Midfielders often cover the most distance of all the players on the field in a game. Professional midfielders often run, jog, and walk more than 6 miles (10 km) in a match. Some of this ground is covered with the ball at their feet, but most of it is "off the ball" simply to get in good positions and track opposing players.

MIDFIELD SETUPS

There are many kinds of midfielders, and they play at different positions on the field. Central midfielders tend to stay more in the center of the pitch, getting involved in the action in the middle, and avoiding drifting to the side of the pitch. Wide midfielders, who are also called wingers, usually play along the side of the field, using their speed and endurance to run up and down the sidelines.

Midfielders also differ based on the offensive and defensive roles they play. Attacking midfielders are mainly involved in passing and setting up chances to score. Defensive midfielders mostly try to win the ball from their opponents, intercept passes, and make safe passes to their teammates.

DIAMOND MIDFIELD

One common midfield formation is known as the diamond or diamond four. The four midfielders in this setup are arranged in a diamond shape. Two midfielders play wide — to the left and the right. The two central midfielders are split between attacking and defending positions.

Of course, there is so much action in a game of soccer that the players in a diamond midfield must move all over the field, so these positions are not completely fixed. But it's important that the players in the diamond move up and down the pitch as a unit, with the diamond shape more or less intact.

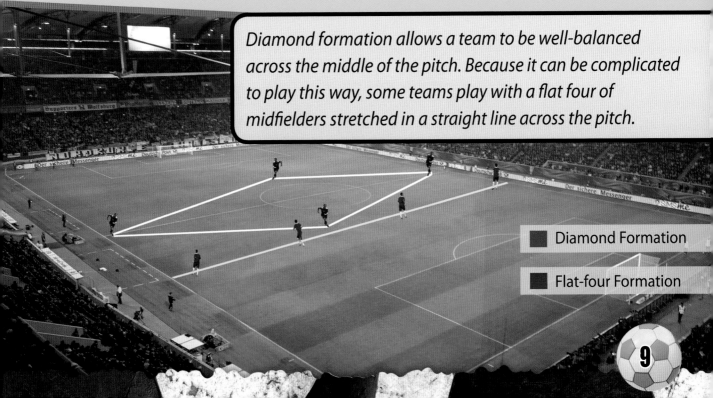

Diamond formation allows a team to be well-balanced across the middle of the pitch. Because it can be complicated to play this way, some teams play with a flat four of midfielders stretched in a straight line across the pitch.

■ Diamond Formation

■ Flat-four Formation

MIDFIELDER SKILLS

Midfielders are often the most skilled players on any team. Because they are in the middle of the pitch, they need outstanding foot skills for passing, dribbling, and shooting. Midfielders must have great **vision**, with the ability to recognize the positioning of teammates and opponents who are often moving very fast. Midfielders also need to be very fit because of all the running they must do.

It is very important for a midfielder to make good decisions on the ball. Strong midfielders know when to choose one option over another in the heat of a game.

Midfielders are often the best decision-makers on a team. By making the right choices, a midfielder can successfully move between defense and offense, and can help their team keep possession of the ball.

A key skill for midfielders is knowing how to measure how much space and time is available to execute certain actions on the pitch. By looking around constantly, a midfielder knows whether teammates and opponents are close or far away and how fast they are moving. For this reason, midfielders must always be heads-up players. Playing without looking around often leads to losing the ball under pressure from an opponent's tackle, or failing to see a teammate running into space for a pass.

Soccer fans sometimes say a midfielder has their "head on a swivel" because they are looking around so much.

CENTRAL MIDFIELDERS

It's impossible for a soccer team at any level of the game to be successful without strong central midfielders. Experienced players in this position keep the ball moving from teammate to teammate, and break up the attacks of opposing teams through tackling and intercepting passes. Central midfielders also connect a team's offense and defense, and link passes from the middle of the pitch out to the wings.

On offense, experienced teams try to "play through the middle," meaning they avoid trying to make long passes from defense to the forwards. Instead, they pass from the defenders to the midfielders, who then link with the forwards.

CENTRAL MIDFIELDER SKILLS

Accurate passing is probably the most important skill for a central midfielder. Players in this position must master a range of long and short passes, hitting the ball along the ground and in the air to teammates who are either standing still or on the move. Central midfielders also must have superior dribbling ability, both to beat opponents and to make space for themselves to pass or shoot.

Central midfielders need more than just ball skills, however. They must also be strong tacklers, and able to win the ball by anticipating and intercepting passes.

Central midfielders must be able to head the ball well, and to use their bodies to protect and shield the ball in tight situations. Because they are so crucial to the way a team plays on both offense and defense, central midfielders also need to be vocal leaders on the pitch.

DEFENSIVE MIDFIELDERS

On most teams, at least one midfielder has a primarily defensive role. Defensive midfielders protect the defense by staying just in front of the back line and stopping passes and dribblers there. Once they have done that important job, these players are expected to make good, smart passes to teammates, rather than dribbling past opponents. These defensive midfielders are often called "holding" midfielders because they "hold" the middle of the pitch.

Defensive midfielders use anticipation to intercept and block passes — and try to get possession once they have won the ball.

French midfielder Claude Makélélé was such a dominant defensive midfielder that this role is often called the "Makélélé position." Makélélé played for the French national team, and for top club teams Real Madrid and Chelsea. Surprisingly, Makélélé was quite a small player, but made up for his lack of size with fierce tackling and a fantastic ability to read the game and connect passes to his teammates.

Above all, defensive midfielders need to know how to tackle and intercept passes. Experienced players in this position time their tackles expertly to avoid **fouling**, and try to retain possession of the ball once they have won it. Defensive midfielders also need to be able to dribble out of tight situations, and to head the ball clear of danger. Finally, these players need to know how to make many short and long passes to teammates.

Defensive midfielders are able to read opponents who are just about to release a pass, and know how to step in front of the player they are guarding at just the right time. This timing is crucial because a missed interception can allow an opponent lots of space to run in on goal!

CENTRAL ATTACKING MIDFIELDERS

With an array of crafty dribbling, skilled passing, and lethal shooting, the central attacking midfielder is usually the most creative player on a team. This position is actually a combination of a forward and midfielder, because the player there often occupies a position very far up the pitch. These players often provide the most assists to set up goals on a team.

A team's central attacking midfielder may be called the number 10 because these players often wear that shirt number.

Midfielders come in all sizes — from tiny to huge — and have all kinds of skill sets. Because the position is so varied, all kinds of players can succeed in the midfield, from tricky dribblers to **ball winners** to speedy wingers. There is as much room for a midfielder who loves to pass as there is for one who loves to tackle and take part in physical play. Of course, some midfielders like to do all of these things in one game!

CENTRAL MIDFIELDER SKILLS

To play the central attacking midfielder position, a player needs many offensive skills. These include outstanding passing and skilled dribbling at high speeds. These players must be experts at reading the game, especially when it comes time to understand how opposing defenses are set up — and how to get through them! Central attacking midfielders must also be able to make a transition quickly, from receiving the ball to making fast decisions to set up teammates.

Many midfielders take the corner kick for their team. Some even score a goal while doing so.

WIDE MIDFIELDERS

Some of the most exciting players on a soccer pitch are the wide midfielders, who set up along the left and right sidelines. Often called wingers because of this positioning, these players use the wide areas to dribble past opponents and cut inside toward the goal in an attempt to score. They also launch aerial **crosses** and passes on the ground to assist their teammates. Many teams will look to pass the ball out to their wingers as a way of starting an attack.

> Wingers must be able to move the ball accurately, whether they are passing along the ground or crossing the ball from well outside the goal area onto the heads of waiting teammates.

When Spain dominated world soccer by winning the European Championship in 2008, the World Cup in 2010, and the Euros again in 2012, they did it with a short-passing, receive-and-move style called "tiki-taka." Small, quick, and precise midfielders were at the heart of this system which totally confused opponents who could not get control of the ball as Spain continually passed it around them.

Wide midfielders have an important job defensively as well. They are usually called upon to shut down opposing wingers or wide defenders trying to press up the pitch to attack. In fact, many coaches demand that their midfield wingers play a dual role in attacking and defending as part of the total team strategy. That means that midfield wingers not only have to be speedy, but also must possess great endurance so that they can run up and down the field the entire game.

In addition to great pace and endurance, wingers must have strong dribbling skills to beat defenders.

BOX-TO-BOX MIDFIELDERS

Box-to-box midfielders combine all the best qualities of all the other types of midfielders. The name for this position comes from the fact that these players cover a huge amount of ground on the pitch, from one penalty box to the other. A mix of attacking and defensive midfielders, these players must have amazing endurance to get up and down the field. They must be superb passers and committed to tackling and intercepting passes.

Because of their importance to a team in the middle of the pitch, box-to-box midfielders need endurance, good composure, and a steady head on the pitch.

Box-to-box midfielders need to be strong tacklers and ball winners. They are experts at knowing exactly when to make a move to win the ball. They avoid lunging in on opponents and making it easy for attackers to dribble past them.

Because being a box-to-box midfielder demands so much of a player, many teams do not use them. However, the ones that do often find that with their energy and leadership, players in this position are crucial to a team's success.

DEEP-LYING MIDFIELDERS

Some soccer coaches make use of players called deep-lying midfielders, sometimes known as playmakers. Although they set up in roughly the same part of the pitch as the defensive midfielder, these players drop back to receive the ball in an attempt to begin offensive play from deep in their own half of the field, using short and long passing and dribbling to open up space for themselves. If a team has a strong deep-lying midfielder, it's not unusual for the entire offense to revolve around them.

Some playmakers are known by nicknames, such as "director," "architect," or "orchestrator," because of the way they seem to create an entire offense around their individual game.

PLAYMAKING SKILLS

By far the most important skill of a deep-lying midfielder is passing. These players must be able to make accurate long passes to their teammates that are easy to control. They also need to complete shorter passes along the ground with pinpoint accuracy. A big part of being successful in this position is knowing which passes to attempt based on the position of opposing players, and when dribbling past them is a more effective plan.

In addition to this excellent knowledge of soccer strategy, playmakers must also be great communicators. They must call for the ball often, letting teammates know they want to receive a pass.

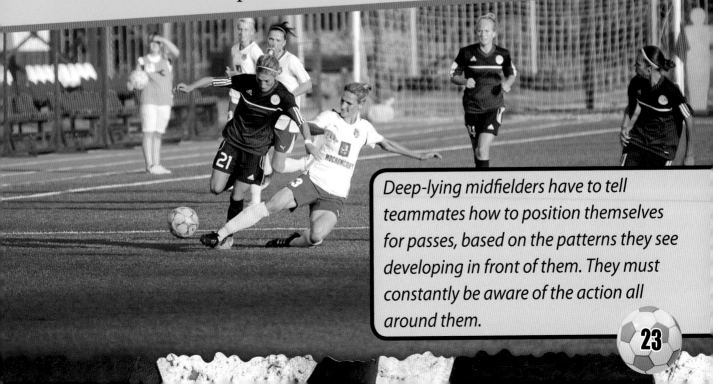

Deep-lying midfielders have to tell teammates how to position themselves for passes, based on the patterns they see developing in front of them. They must constantly be aware of the action all around them.

THE ROLE OF A HEAD COACH

In professional soccer, head coaches are sometimes called managers. Head coaches decide what strategy a team will use and what formation it will play. They also pick the starting 11 players for a game, and which substitutes will come into each game. Most head coaches are very active on the sidelines during games, yelling instructions to players.

Many coaches rely on midfielders to be the main players to help them carry out their game plans. Since time-outs are not allowed in soccer, midfielders often act as second coaches on the pitch, communicating with teammates about the finer points of the game.

Head coaches also work hard at training their team. Along with their assistant coaches, head coaches decide what aspects of the game to work on in training — whether it is individual ball skills, passing, defending, or team tactics. Head coaches also help players work on fitness and individual skills, both on the field and in the gym and weight rooms. At the higher levels of the game, head coaches will often watch videos of opposing teams before games to study their strengths and weaknesses.

Coaches help players get motivated to train and play games. They also help players learn about the importance of a healthy diet, proper sleep and rest, and doing well in school and the community.

THE BEST MIDFIELDERS

Famous midfielders of the past include Johann Cruy of the Netherlands who revolutionized attacking midfield play in the 1970s, scoring and setting up goals. French midfielder Louisa Cadamuro is a legend for her ability to dribble, pass, and score. Michelle Akers is famous for playing two positions — striker and defensive midfielder. She was named a FIFA Player of the Century!

Andrea "The Architect" Pirlo (left) defines the playmaker role. He has played for the Italian national team, AC Milan, Juventus, and New York FC. Paul Pogba of France (right) is over six feet (nearly 2 m) tall! He's a forceful player on both offense and defense.

Many soccer fans consider Xavi Hernandez of Spain and Barcelona to be the greatest midfielder in professional men's soccer history. His control, passing skills, and ability to read the game are remarkable. Under his leadership, Spain won the 2008 European Championships, the 2010 World Cup, and the European title again in 2012!

Many great midfielders are playing the game today, too. They include France's Ngolo Kante who dominates opponents with his tackling and pass interceptions. American Michael Bradley pulls the strings for the US national team and Toronto FC in Major League Soccer. Spanish midfielder Andres Iniesta is a dribbling and passing genius known as "El Cerebro" — or, "The Brain."

Mesut Ozil of Germany (left) is a classic number 10 with an unbelievable arsenal of passing and dribbling skills who also plays for the English club Arsenal. Carli Lloyd (right) is the powerful midfield force at the heart of the dominant US Women's National Team.

BE A GOOD SPORT

Soccer is called "the beautiful game" for a good reason. Sportsmanship is at the heart of soccer, and in addition to the official rules of the game, there are many unwritten rules about etiquette that are unique to soccer. These include helping an opponent who has fallen down up off the pitch, not running up a big score against a weaker team, and kicking the ball out of bounds when an opponent is injured so he or she can receive treatment.

Referees show a yellow warning card when players have been unsporting or disrespectful. If players receive a second yellow card, they must leave the match.

RESPECTING THE REFEREES

Just like players and coaches, referees want to do the best they can. Because they are human, referees can and do make mistakes. Players, coaches, fans, and parents should always show respect for referees and their assistant linesmen. It is always poor sportsmanship to yell at officials and to dispute the calls they have made. At the youth levels of soccer, many referees are also young people themselves, and need to be supported in the decisions they make.

RESPECT

Respect for opponents helps the game go smoothly, and it is always likely that a team receiving respectful treatment will also give back that respect. Even though it is important for soccer players to give 100 percent effort in games and training, this should never be more important than showing respect for teammates and opponents. After all, they are trying just as hard as you are.

Respect should extend to coaches, parents, and fans. In youth soccer, many people play an important in the success of individuals and teams — so it never hurts to give a big thanks to the people who help and support you in developing your skills and building your love of the game.

GLOSSARY

ball winners Players who specialize in defensive play, especially taking the ball away from an opponent through tackling or intercepting a pass.

crosses Long passes, delivered through the air, from the wing into the goal area.

formation The setup of a soccer team, in which the 10 outfield players are arranged on the pitch.

fouling Breaking the rules of soccer when coming into contact with another player, such as tripping, shoving, or kicking an opponent.

pitch The soccer field.

reading (a game or player) Understanding exactly what is happening on the pitch and using that knowledge to anticipate what will happen next.

tackling To attempt to win the ball from an opposing player.

vision The ability to recognize patterns of play on the soccer pitch.

FOR MORE INFORMATION

FURTHER READING

Crisfield, Deborah W. *The Everything Kids' Soccer Book: Rules, Techniques, and More About Your Favorite Sport!* Adams Media, 2015.

Jökulsson, Illugi. *Stars of World Soccer*. Abbeville Kids, 2015.

Lloyd, Carli, and Wayne Coffey. *All Heart: My Dedication and Determination to Become One of Soccer's Best*. HMH Books for Young Readers, 2016.

WEBSITES

Due to the changing nature of Internet links, PowerKids Press has developed an online list of websites related to the subject of this book. This site is updated regularly. Please use this link to access the list:

www.powerkidslinks.com/ss/midfielder

INDEX